Time for Ferrets

Time for Ferrets

LILO HESS

Charles Scribner's Sons · New York

Photographs page 17 courtesy U.S. Fish & Wildlife Service.
Top, Luther C. Goldman; Bottom, Donald Hammer.

Charles Scribner's Sons Books for Young Readers
Macmillan Publishing Company
866 Third Avenue, New York, NY 10022
Collier Macmillan Canada, Inc.

Printed in the United States of America
First Edition   10 9 8 7 6 5 4 3 2 1

Library of Congress Cataloging-in-Publication Data
Hess, Lilo.   Time for ferrets.
Includes index.
Summary: Text and photographs detail the life and behavior of ferrets.
1. Ferrets as pets—Juvenile literature.
2. Ferrets—Anecdotes—Juvenile literature.   [1. Ferrets]   I. Title.
SF459.F47H47   1987   636′.974′447   87-9765
ISBN 0-684-18788-4

Early one morning Lucy was awakened by the loud barking of her dogs. She had eleven stray and abandoned dogs living on her farm, because all the runs at the Animal Rescue Shelter, where she was a volunteer worker, were full. One of Lucy's jobs at the shelter was to find homes for all the different kinds of animals that were brought there. When the shelter was full she took the animals to her farm until she could place them into good homes.

Lucy put on her robe and went out to investigate. She expected to find a box of abandoned puppies or kittens, but instead she saw a wire cage with three lively ferrets inside.

5

Ferrets are the latest fad in pets. Apartment dwellers like them because of their small size. Females are about fourteen inches long and weigh one and one-half to two pounds. The slightly larger males are about sixteen inches long and seldom weigh more than three and one-half pounds. Elderly people like them because they are clean, quiet companions. The only noises they make are soft grunts, squeaks, or chatters. Young people like them because they are easy to care for and are full of fun. Everybody likes ferrets because they are unusual pets. Stores sell them as fast as they can get them. One breeding farm sells about 1,200 baby ferrets a month and claims that they could sell many more. Owners are starting to form ferret clubs, and ferret shows are being held. Unfortunately, many people buy the animals as cute babies and get tired of them after a short time. Ferrets, however, can live ten to twelve years.

Lucy took the three newcomers to another part of the farm where a few homeless rabbits, guinea pigs, two other ferrets, and an injured squirrel were housed. Although Lucy advises people who handle a strange ferret for the first time to wear protective gloves until they know that the animal is really tame, she herself reached into the cage without gloves and pulled out the first ferret. She grasped it with her fingers underneath its front legs, and she supported its rear with her other hand. It was a male with a white head and creamy yellow body fur tipped with some black. His feet and tail were dark brown. He was very tame, but dirty and smelly. Lucy named him Jiggs.

The other two were females of various shades of brown with dark facial masks. They were also tame and friendly. One of them was pregnant and seemed to be close to giving birth. She was named Maggie. The other, a sleek lively animal, was named Bandit. They all were about two years old. The male was put into a cage by himself while the two females shared the adjoining one.

The homemade cages were roomy and sturdy. They were about five feet long, three feet wide, and two feet high. Three sides were made of welded one-by-one-inch wire mesh. The fourth side, which contained the door, and the roof were made of plywood. The wire on the bottom of the cage was one-by-two-inch mesh to let the waste fall through. All the cages were up on legs to make clean-up underneath easier and to protect the ferrets from crawling or hopping pests. Indoor cages can be made of wire or wood. A wooden cage should have one side made of wire so that the animal can see out and for ventilation.

8

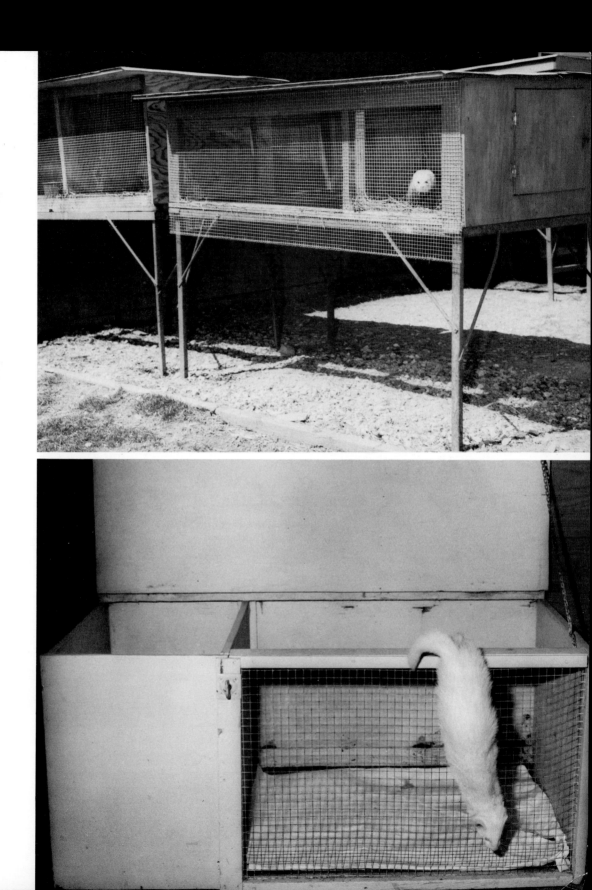

Since ferrets sleep a lot and like to curl up in a dark, warm place, each cage should have a sleeping box. The box can be made of wood or plastic. It can be plain or fancy, and it can be

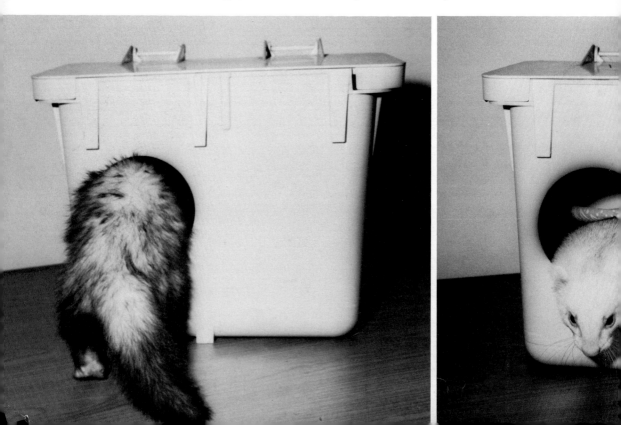

free-standing or attached to the cage. It should have an entrance hole about three inches in diameter in the front or on one side. The top should be hinged or removable so that it can be opened for cleaning or checking on the animal. It is advisable to have a safety catch, hook, or other fastener on the outside of the lid; otherwise the nosy ferrets will push it open from inside. In the box, ferrets like to snuggle and burrow into fragrant hay, soft towels, or pieces of blankets. Ferrets never soil their sleeping quarters, but they will drag in food scraps, so the box should be checked every few days and cleaned once a week.

If a ferret has to live outdoors in cold climates, it should have another ferret for company and warmth during the winter months. A male and a female or two females can easily be kept together, but two males might fight unless they have been raised together.

Lucy gave the new animals food and water and then left them to get used to their surroundings. In the afternoon she took them out to cut their toe nails. The nails were so long that the ferrets might scratch and hurt themselves or each other. Nail clippers like the ones used for dogs or cats worked well, and the little animals did not object. Afterward Lucy brushed all the loose dirt out of their fur and then dusted them with flea powder made for dogs. She intended to give Jiggs and Bandit a bath in a few days. She did not want to bathe Maggie, the pregnant female, because the handling might have upset her and caused her to lose her babies.

Jiggs was very interested in the farm animals he could see from his cage, and he craned his neck to look around the corner to see more. The next day Lucy took him out for a walk so he could meet some of the animals. But the visit was not very successful. Lucy put Jiggs on a little nylon harness, which is specially made for ferrets and is available in pet shops. He walked very well on the lead. He wanted to go close to the sheep, goats, chickens, and ducks to smell and play with them, but they were afraid and ran away as soon as he approached. Not

even the dogs wanted to be friendly. A doberman called Marty came over briefly and sniffed, but as soon as he got the ferret's scent, he bolted away. Usually ferrets get along well with household pets. Lucy picked up Jiggs and was about to return him to his cage when a young steer trotted up to the fence to see him. Jiggs was scared and turned his head as if he wanted no part of the steer, but then, before Lucy could stop him, he nipped the steer on its moist black nose. The startled 1,000-pound steer galloped away, snorting and whimpering. That in turn frightened Jiggs even more. He leaped out of Lucy's arms and dove into a clump of hay that had been spilled on the ground. Lucy had to pull hard on his lead to drag him out.

Lucy decided to keep Jiggs and Maggie on her farm and to find a good family to adopt Bandit. Lucy was very selective about who could adopt one of her animals. The two ferrets already residing at her farm had been abused and mishandled before they came to her and therefore were not friendly and trustworthy enough to make good pets. Ferrets are often bred only to make money and without regard to their temperament. Nasty individuals often have bad-tempered offspring. The early care of the babies is very important in shaping their future disposition. They must be handled often and kindly so that they learn to like and trust humans. People buying pet ferrets should deal with a breeder who can show them the babies' parents.

In former times almost all pet ferrets were albinos, which means they were white and had red or pink eyes. Later they were bred in many different colors. Sable, a brown color, is the most common; other popular colors are gray, silver, cinnamon, siamese, chocolate, platinum, and even spotted. The rarer the

color, the higher the price. Some ferrets have dark facial masks, like Bandit and Maggie; others have only partial masks or no masks at all, like Jiggs. Feet, legs, and tail can be brown, black, or light in color.

A pet ferret with black feet, though, is not the same as the almost extinct wild American black-footed ferret, *Mustela nigripes*. The color of this wild ferret is usually reddish brown, and it has black feet, a black mask, and a black tail tip. It spends most of its time underground, making its home in the burrows of prairie dogs in the plains and prairies of the western United States. Although it eats various small mammals, prairie dogs make up about 90 percent of its diet. Prairie dogs are small

rodents that live in large underground colonies. Because they competed for food with grass-feeding livestock, man declared war on prairie dogs, poisoning them and destroying their habitats. As a result, the wild ferret almost vanished as well. It was believed for some time that this animal indeed had become extinct, but a few years ago a small colony of about 128 individuals was discovered in Wyoming. Unfortunately, a plague destroyed most of them. The Game and Fish Department in Wyoming has now decided to capture all the remaining wild ferrets in this colony and start a breeding program in captivity. If successful, the offspring will be reestablished in the wild. It is also hoped that a few other wild ferret colonies still exist somewhere in the vast Western Plains and that the captive animals are not really the last of their species.

After the new ferrets on Lucy's farm had been there for several days, they got a bath in the bathroom sink. Bandit wriggled and squirmed and obviously did not enjoy the water, but Jiggs loved it. A mild shampoo was used and he licked the soapy foam. Many ferrets will chew on a cake of soap as if it were candy. Different theories have been expressed to explain this habit, one being that individuals who chew soap might lack fat in their diet. When all the soap was rinsed off, Jiggs jumped out of the water onto a dry towel. As if he had done this before, he slid over it, rubbed himself dry, and then crawled into its folds to keep warm. Lucy gave him a final rub and then began to clean his ears. She dipped a cotton swab into baby oil and carefully cleaned out all the dark, waxy matter. Jiggs objected strongly but did not bite nor make a sound. After he and Bandit were finished, they got a teaspoonful of yogurt as a reward. Like

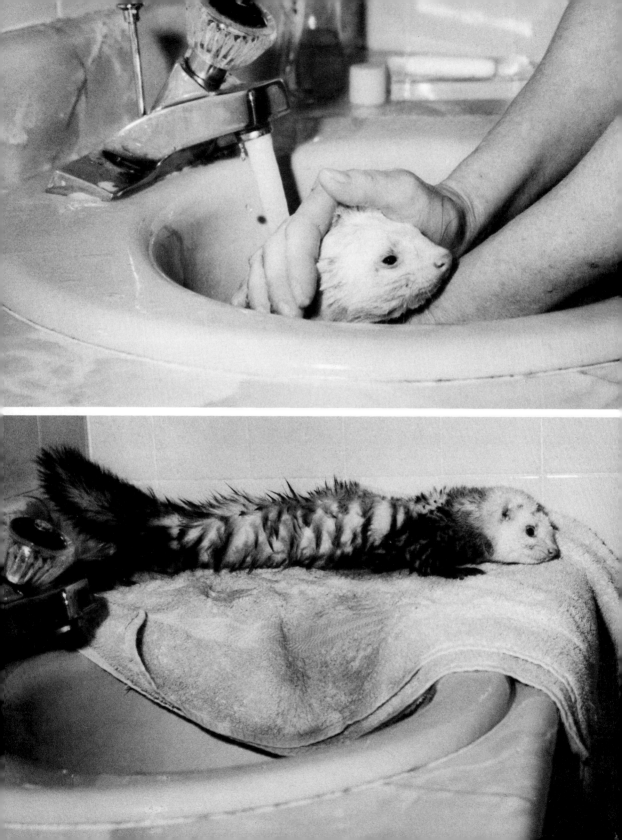

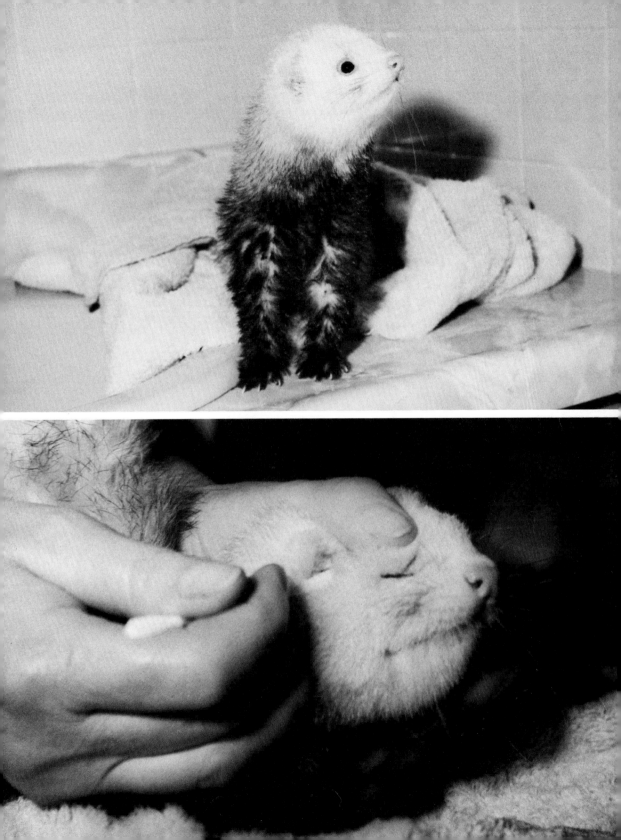

most ferrets they loved this treat. Because it was cold outside, they were kept in a small indoor cage for a few hours before being returned to their outdoor cages.

Lucy also gave the three ferrets distemper shots, because she did not know if they had received that very important yearly immunization in their previous home. Ferrets are very susceptible to distemper and will die if they contract it. Some veterinarians will also give ferrets a rabies shot. The ferrets should be at least six months old before this shot is given, because younger animals might die or get the disease from the treatment. Ferrets are also very susceptible to the human cold.

The three ferrets adjusted very quickly to their new life. They were handled often, groomed regularly, and got plenty of nourishing food. They are carnivores, or meat eaters, and must have a high-protein diet. They seem to do well on dry cat food and some canned cat or dog food. From time to time they should get a little fresh raw meat such as hamburger or a chicken neck. They also like to gnaw on bones. Some individuals like cooked or raw fish, vegetables, and fruits. Each ferret has its own preferences, and owners will learn quickly what they are. Most ferrets seem to love milk, yogurt, and ice cream, but too many milk products might give them diarrhea. They need no special vitamins if they are fed a good diet, but a few drops of a commercial skin and coat conditioner added to their food two or three times a week will keep their fur soft and shiny. Ferrets are so active that they burn up food very quickly; therefore it is best to feed them twice a day or leave dry food in the cage for the entire day. Uneaten moist food should be removed since it spoils quickly. Most ferrets will not overeat, but if a pet puts on too much weight, it should get less food and more exercise.

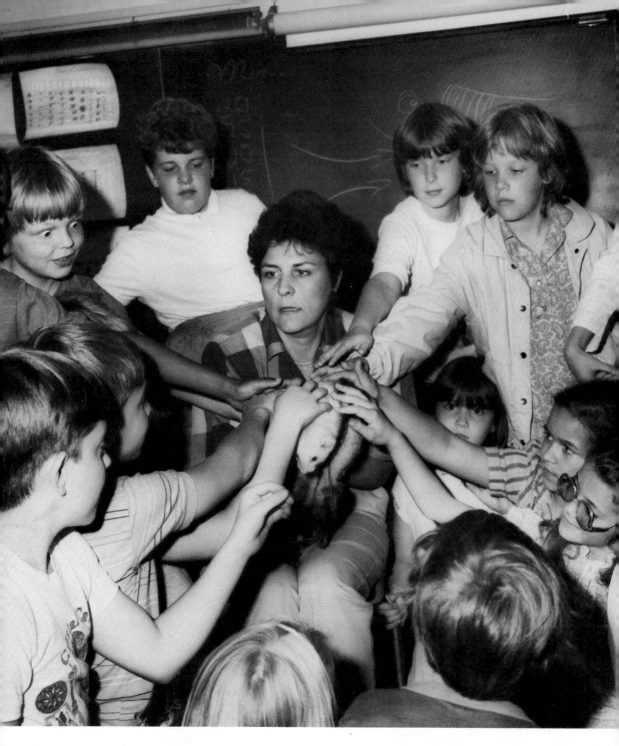

Lucy decided that Jiggs was an ideal pet to take to the local schools so that children could learn about this interesting animal. A few days later Jiggs made his first appearance in a classroom. The teacher told the students to be quiet and gentle to prevent Jiggs from getting scared. All the boys and girls petted Jiggs, and he seemed to love the attention. The teacher asked if anyone knew what kind of an animal a ferret was, and to what other animals it was related. Some children identified it correctly as a type of mink or weasel. The teacher told them that ferrets indeed belong to the weasel family. The ferret's family name is *Mustelidae,* the genus is *Mustela,* and the species is *putorius furo.* Its cousins are the skunk, otter, mink, badger, wolverine, and polecat. But the ferret we have as pets does not occur in the wild. It is a domesticated animal. Its exact origin is still disputed. Some people say that it has been bred from the wild European polecat *(Mustela putorius),* which looks very much like the pet animal we have today, and from which it gets its name. Others think that it was bred from the Asiatic or steppe polecat *(Mustela eversmanni).*

Ferrets were used and bred by the Egyptians as early as the fourth century B.C. Later the Romans and the Chinese had tame ferrets that were used to catch mice, rats, and other pests.

Eventually, hunting rabbits with the help of ferrets became a very popular sport in England, Scotland, and a few other European countries. The ferret was sent into the rabbits' underground burrows to drive them out into the open where the hunter could kill them. When the hunt was over, the hunter called his ferret back by ringing a little bell or making some other sound to which the ferret had been trained to respond. Sometimes a ferret would not obey and stay in one of the cozy, dark rabbit chambers and go to sleep. There was not much the hunter could do. He could wait until the ferret woke up and surfaced, or he could send a second ferret into the burrow to chase the first one out. Some hunters put a long leash or line on their ferrets so that they could pull the animals out, but because the line often got entangled on underground roots or rocks, this method was unsatisfactory. In most countries today, hunting with ferrets has been outlawed. We still use the expression "to ferret something out" to describe a thorough search by cunning methods.

In 1875 the animal became very popular in the United States. In rural areas people still remember the ferret man, who came to rid buildings of mice and rats. He would bring a few ferrets in a box and release them in barns, basements, or other out-buildings to hunt. Sometimes he left them overnight. When people complained of mice rustling inside the walls of their homes, the ferret man closed up all escape holes on the base of the wall except one. The ferrets entered the wall through this hole. Soon one could hear them hunting. When the job was done, the ferret man rang his bell, and the ferrets returned to their cage. Ferrets were also used in some large cities to destroy rats that lived in underground sewer pipes.

At the turn of the century, backyard breeders and breeding farms sprang up all over the country. Today, several states require special permits to keep ferrets, and some states prohibit keeping them at all. They fear that lost or escaped individuals might breed in the wild and endanger small game and poultry. Ferrets could not survive in cold weather, but in moderate climates they might live. In England and Scotland a few small colonies of feral ferrets, tame animals that have gone wild, have been sighted.

Ferrets and all their cousins have scent glands. Only skunks can spray their musk; they have a range of several yards. Skunks are sometimes called polecats, but their musk is much stronger than that of the true polecats or ferrets. When people keep skunks as pets they have them descented.

Pet ferrets can also have their musk glands surgically removed, and most veterinarians do this operation at the same time that they neuter the animal. During Jiggs' classroom visit, the teacher asked the class to smell the animal's musky odor. She said that males have a much stronger odor than females and that the musk glands of animals used for breeding are usually left intact. Some of the children liked the scent; others were repelled by it.

One girl asked Lucy if ferrets really made good and gentle pets. She said Jiggs' teeth looked very big and sharp. Lucy said that was an important question, because so many different opinions are voiced about it. Some people feel that they are bad pets; others claim that they are just wonderful. What is the truth? Most ferrets get very tame and friendly when handled properly, but they are pets for older children only. Babies, toddlers, and preschoolers should never be allowed to handle a ferret unsupervised. Ferrets are easily startled by noise or rough play. They have poor eyesight and might mistake a quick movement for a threatening gesture and bite in self-defense. No ferret should ever be put into a crib with a baby—not for fun, not even for a minute. But for responsible children a lively, playful ferret can be a good companion. Like a puppy, a very young ferret might nip playfully, but it responds to training and will learn the meaning of the word "no."

After the talk everyone petted Jiggs good-bye and watched as the tired ferret curled up in its box and went to sleep before Lucy could close the lid.

Sometimes Bandit or one of Lucy's other ferrets, an albino named Daisy, were taken to the schools. One student, ten-year-old Matt, was so taken with Bandit that he asked Lucy if he could buy her. Lucy said that if he could get his parents' permission, and if he could prove that he could provide a good home for Bandit, he could adopt her.

A few days later Matt and his father visited Lucy's farm. Matt's father was just as enthusiastic as his son about adopting Bandit. Matt put on a pair of old gloves to handle Bandit, who

seemed to like this new friend and sniffed him all over. She stayed in his arms for a little while, then she wanted to get down and investigate the room. Matt's father had a briefcase that he had put on a chair after arriving. Bandit discovered that the briefcase was partially open, and she pushed and poked until she could crawl inside. She went in and out several times, then curled up on the bottom among the papers and went to sleep. Lucy agreed that they could adopt Bandit and gave them instructions on how to care for a ferret that would have free run of the house for most of the day.

She especially warned them that ferrets have a knack for disappearing and staying out of sight for hours. She suggested that they put a little bell around Bandit's neck so they would always know where she was hiding. When it was time to leave, Bandit was still asleep in the briefcase, and Matt transported her to her new home in it.

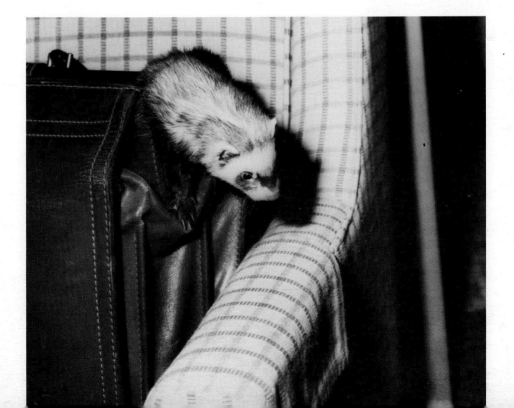

Two weeks later Lucy got a letter from Matt. He wrote:

"Bandit did not wake up until we had been home for more than one hour. She immediately investigated the house. She jumped up on the sofa and played hide and seek with me, hiding behind the pillows. When I caught her she made little gurgling sounds. She played with her new toys and tried to make friends with our cat. But the cat hissed and Bandit ran away. At first she did not know how to get up the staircase in the house, but she soon learned to run up and down it very fast. After an hour she got tired and could not stop yawning. We put her into her cage, gave her food and water, and watched her rearrange her blankets in her sleeping box. She slept all that evening and probably most of the next day. When I came home

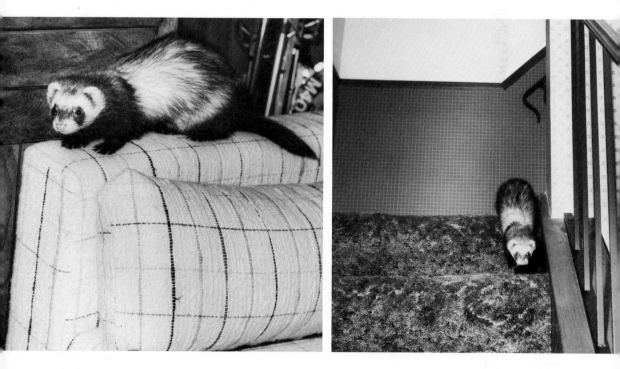

from school she wanted to play. We put a pan filled with cat litter into her cage, just the way you told us to do, but she soiled a corner of the cage. My dad put some of the droppings into the litter pan so that she would understand what it was for. That worked and she has used it ever since. I put a second litter pan in a corner of the living room, because she spends a lot of time playing there. I clean it out every day so that it does not smell bad.

"It was funny when Bandit discovered where the cookies are kept. Now she steals them whenever she thinks no one is watching. She found a dark corner upstairs in my dad's study where she hides her treasures. Cookies, toys, bottlecaps, spoons, and pencils all end up there. She likes the kitchen sponge and

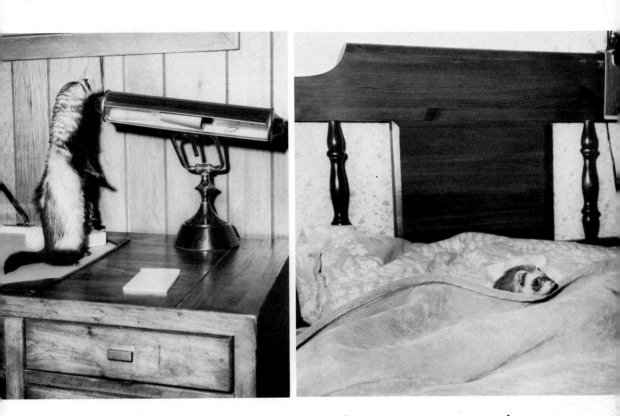

brings it to her hiding place no matter how many times we take it away from her. I check every few days to make sure she hasn't hidden any food there. Bandit also likes to play with all the things on my dad's desk, and if the filing cabinet is open, she tries to make a cozy nest among the papers. But her very favorite place is my parents' bed. They had to take the bedspread away and put an old blanket on the bed so that Bandit can roll and jump on it and tunnel underneath without hurting anything. She does not really go to sleep in the bed, but she tries. She inspects every drawer and crawls under every chest, and we have to be careful not to lock her in somewhere. Next week we will get a little bell for her.

"We had a little excitement the other day. We took her outdoors and just put a cat collar and leash on her. Suddenly she
slipped out of the collar. Our whole family came out to stand
guard. Bandit had fun investigating every hole. She turned over
leaves, sticks, and stones. The woodlot behind our house has
some hollow logs lying about, and Bandit ran in and out of
them. When we wanted to go back, I squeaked one of her rub-
ber toys and she came running to me. But before she went inside, she made a little side trip to the drain pipe on our house
and played and rolled around in it. Then she came inside to see
what was for dinner. From now on we will use her harness. We
all love her and I am proud that she is my pet."

Lucy was delighted that Bandit had such a happy home.

Now Maggie, the pregnant female, was ready to give birth. Ferrets give birth about forty-two days after they have conceived. The female usually comes into heat, the period during which she can be bred, from March to August, when there are about sixteen hours of daylight. If she is not bred she will stay in heat for the entire time. Some pets seem unable to come out of heat by themselves and need medication to terminate the cycle. During this time the vulva is greatly enlarged, which makes the animal prone to infections that can be fatal. The female can also develop anemia, a shortage of iron in the blood. If she is not used for breeding, she should be spayed.

The courtship of ferrets looks very rough. The male throws his mate about, pushes her to the ground, shakes her, and gives the impression of hurting her. As savage as it might seem, this behavior seems to have a soothing effect on the female. She becomes submissive and relaxed. Mating may be quick or last for several hours.

Lucy had fixed a maternity cage for Maggie in the basement of the house. Instead of the usual nest box, Lucy put in a little basket with soft clean towels. This way she could better observe the babies. Maggie liked the basket and pulled the towels all around herself. She consumed almost double her normal ration of food, and she was shedding her coat, which is a normal process right before or after giving birth, or whelping, as it is sometimes called.

Maggie had six healthy babies, three males and three females. The babies were blind and deaf at birth, and they were two to three inches long. They looked pink with a thin, fine covering of white fuzz. As they grew, the white fur became longer and denser. Regardless of what color your ferrets will eventually be,

39

all are white for the first three weeks of their lives. Maggie was
a devoted mother and kept her babies clean and content.

After the third week the babies had grown so much that Lucy
decided to give them a little extra food. The supplement to their
mother's milk was a commercial milk replacer formula, available
in pet shops. Lucy gave them each a few drops of the formula
with an eye dropper three times a day. Maggie was so protective

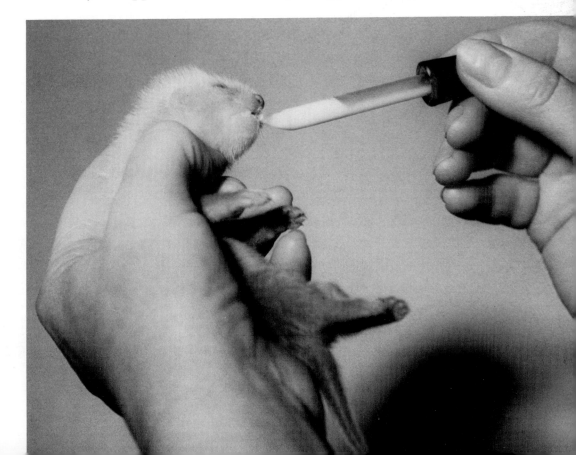

of her young that she had to be confined in a separate cage while the babies were fed. As each baby finished its feeding, it was placed on a towel where it slept. This was done to keep count of the babies that had been fed. After the feeding Maggie was released. She rushed to her babies, picked them up in her mouth, and carried each one back to the nest.

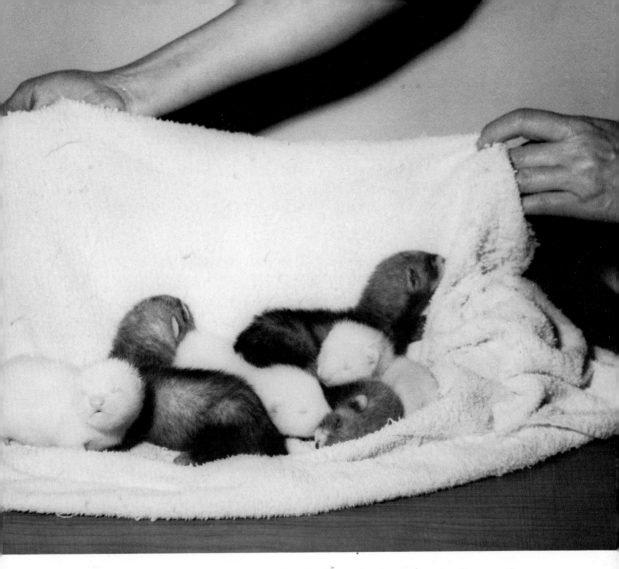

At the age of four weeks the babies had sharp little teeth. They were fed the milk formula mixed with pablum and strained beef or liver baby food. The color of three of the babies had changed to soft gray. Under the still-closed eyelids a dark spot was visible. This meant that they would have dark eyes. The other three babies were still white, and their eyes showed no dark pigment. They were albinos and their eyes would be red.

At the age of five weeks the babies could hear, and their eyes were open. The fur of the three gray babies had turned into a warm brown color. All six ate by themselves, although they got as much food on their faces as into their stomachs. They became very active. They investigated their surroundings, played with the toys Lucy had given them, and wrestled and pushed each other in mock fights.

At six weeks of age the babies were weaned and taken from their mother, and the following week they were ready to live separate lives. At this age ferrets are at their cutest, and Lucy had no trouble finding homes for them. She screened every prospective owner carefully and planned to stay in touch with the ones who adopted the animals. She wanted to be certain that her ferrets would never be mistreated and would always have a happy home.

Index

distemper shots, 22
ferrets:
  bathing of, 12, 18
  behavior of, 10, 11, 31–38
  birth of, 38–39
  black-footed, 16
  buying, 15
  cages for, 8, 10–11, 22, 39, 42
  color of, 15–16, 39–41, 43
  courtship of, 38
  domestication of, 26
  feeding of, 18, 22–23, 39, 41–42, 43, 44
  grooming of, 12
  growth of young, 39–46
  handling of, 7, 15, 28, 29

  harness for, 13, 37
  hunting with, 26–27
  immunization for, 22
  lifespan of, 6
  popularity of, 6
  scent of, 15, 27
  size of, 6
  temperament of, 15
  vitamins for, 23
mink, 25
polecat:
  European, 25
  steppe, 25
prairie dog, 18
rabies shots, 22
weasel, 25